Growing Readers

New Hanover County Public Library

Purchased with
New Hanover County Partnership for Children
and Smart Start Funds

Distributed in the United States by
Smart Apple Media,
1980 Lookout Drive,
North Mankato,
Minnesota 56003

Text copyright © Linda Bygrave
Illustrations copyright © Louise Voce

Consultant: Michael Chinery

ISBN 1-93198-348-8
Library of Congress Control Number 2003102388

Printed in China

I am a Duck

Written By
Linda Bygrave

Illustrated by
Louise Voce

Chrysalis Education

I am a duck.
I like to live near water.

Like all birds, I have feathers
covering my body.
They keep me warm and dry.

You can often see me in parks.
I am usually by the water
because I love to swim.

You have probably heard
the sound I make. What is it?
That's right! "Quack, quack!"

I have short legs and
big webbed feet.

This means that I have skin
between my toes. Look!

Because my legs are so short,
I am not very good at walking.
I waddle from side to side.

But I am a wonderful swimmer.
I use my webbed feet to paddle
along in the water.

I use my wings for flying.
I can even take off from water.
Here I go!

I can land on water too.
I use my webbed feet like brakes.
They slow me down as I land.

I like to keep myself very clean.
I use my beak to clean my feathers,
just like you use a brush or comb.

I spread a special oil on my feathers,
which helps to keep them dry.
The oil comes from near my tail.

I mostly feed on plants in the water.
Sometimes people feed me bread.

To reach the plants under the water,
I tip myself up like this.

I am a mommy duck.
Over there is a daddy duck.
He is called a drake.

His feathers are a different color
from mine. He is showing them to me
because he wants us to have babies.

It is early spring and I have made
a nest of leaves and grass.
I have ten beautiful eggs in my nest.

I have spread soft plants
around the inside of the nest
to make it warm and cozy.

I sit on my eggs for about a month.
Then my ducklings start to hatch out.
Look! Aren't they tiny?

My ducklings are covered
in soft, fluffy feathers called down.
They are very hungry.

My ducklings can swim as soon
as we go into the water.
They follow me in a neat little line.

I say, "Quack, quack!"
They say, "Cheep, cheep!"
This way, we can always find each other.

I must watch my ducklings carefully
and stop big fish and birds
from getting too close to them.

In about six weeks, my ducklings will
be able to fly. It has been a busy day
and it is time for us to rest. Good-bye!